My Big Wipe Clean Handwriting

Cat

I can help you write words

This book belongs to:

_____

(Don't worry if you can't write your name now—you'll be able to once you've finished this book!)

Autumn
Publishing

Pen Control

One way to hold a pen is to grip it between your thumb and index finger. That way, the pen can rest on your middle finger while you write. To begin with, just hold the pen in whatever way feels most comfortable for you.

Practice makes perfect!

Pen Control

Draw a single dot inside each of these circles.

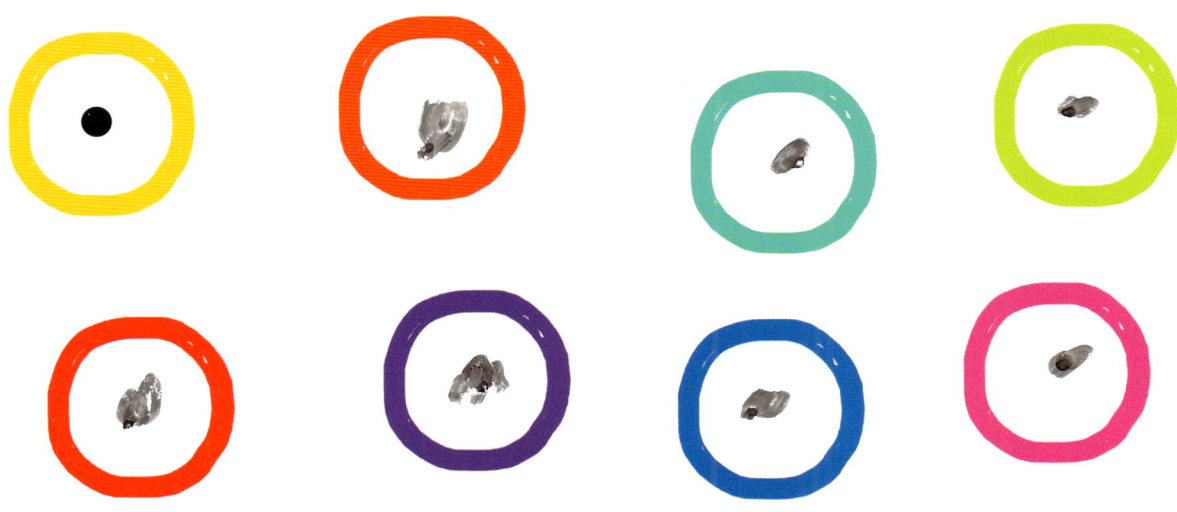

Horizontal Lines

A horizontal line is a straight line that travels across the page.
Hold your pen steady and draw from each dot on the
left to each arrow on the right to create horizontal lines below.

Now draw more horizontal lines here.
Some are short and some are long.

Vertical Lines

A vertical line is a straight line that runs up or down the page. Start with the blue balloon and draw from the dot at the top down to the arrow at the bottom to create vertical lines.

Diagonal Lines

A diagonal line is a straight line that's drawn at a slanted angle. Draw all the way from each of the dots to each of the arrows to create diagonal lines.

Zigzag Lines

A zigzag line is a straight line that moves diagonally up and down across the page. Draw all the way from the dots to each arrow to create zigzag lines.

Wavy Lines

A wavy line is a curved line that moves up and down across the page. Draw all the way from the dots to each arrow to create wavy lines.

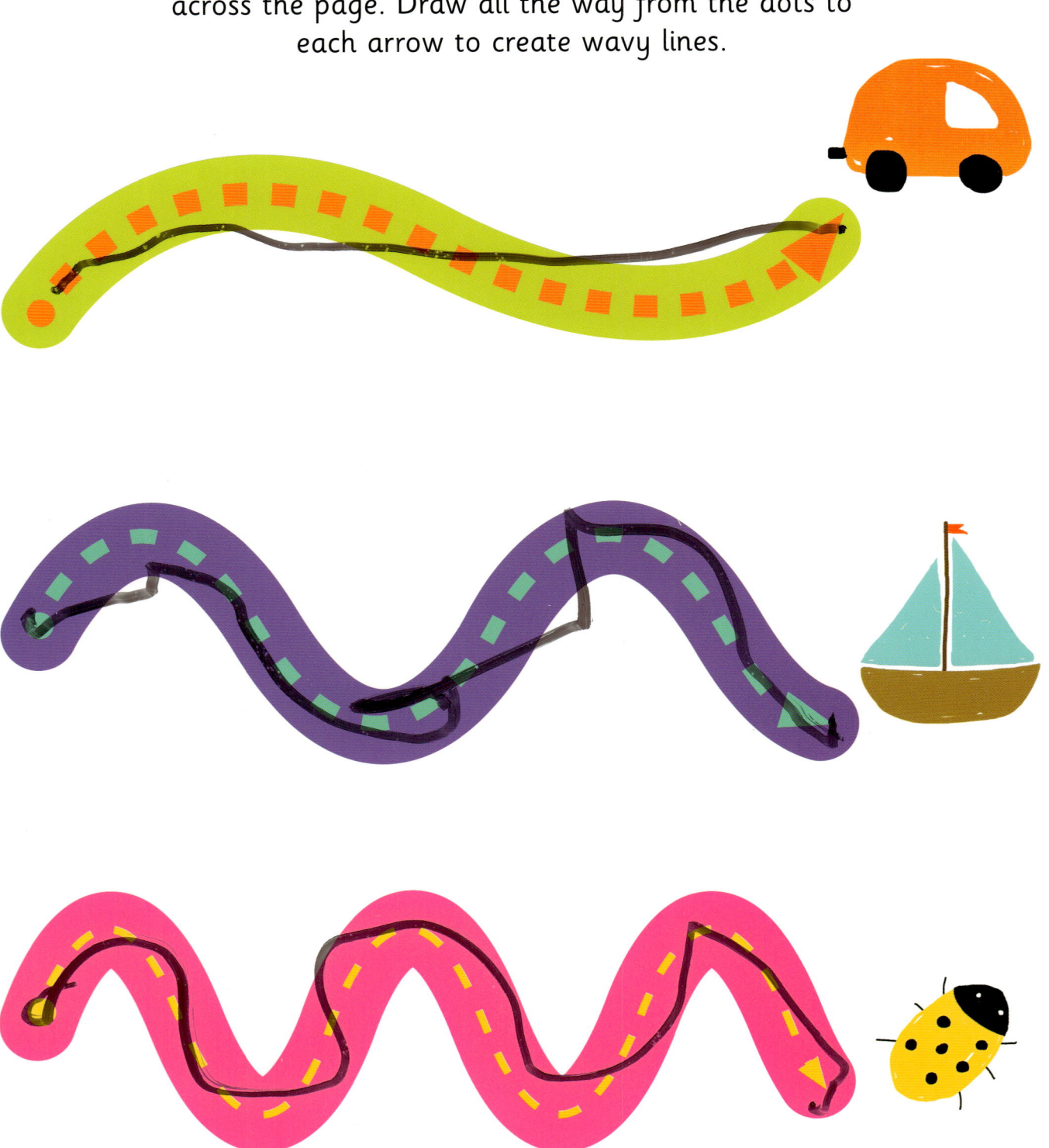

Looped Lines

A looped line is a curved line that travels backward on itself before continuing on. Draw all the way from the dots to each arrow to create looped lines.

Lines Practice

Trace over the lines to draw some candles for this birthday cake. Then, draw some of your own. The first candle has been done for you.

Can you draw a curly tail and straight whiskers on this mouse?

Lines Practice

Trace over the dotted lines with your pen to find out which item belongs to each owl.

Lines Practice

Draw a line through the maze to help Mommy Bird get back to the nest. Be careful not to draw outside the lines.

Lines Practice

Draw a line through the maze to help the cat reach the mouse.
Try your hardest not to draw outside the lines.

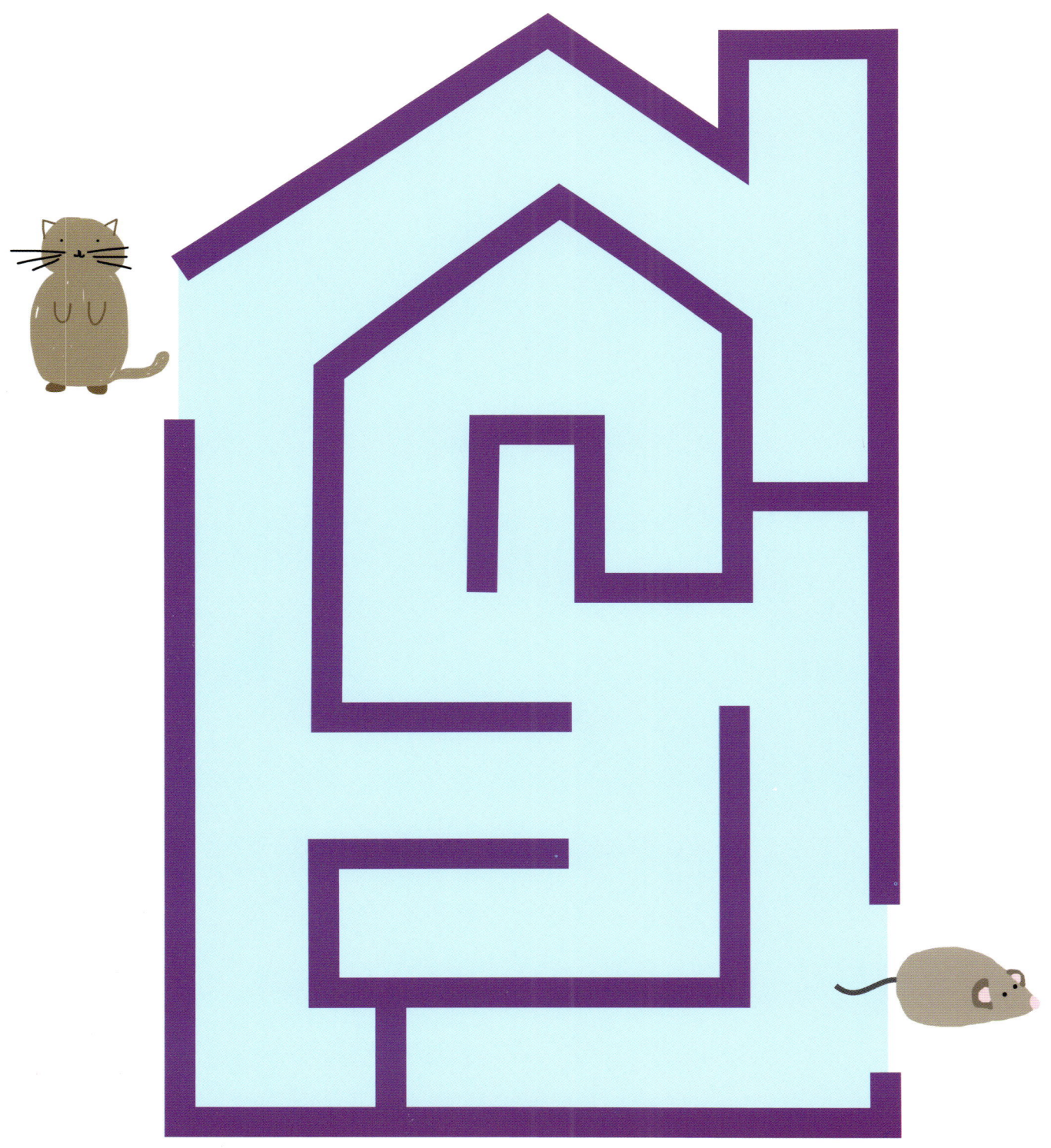

Squares

Draw a line around each of the four sides to create squares below.

Rectangles

Draw a line around each of the four sides to create rectangles below.

Triangles

Draw a line around each of the three sides to create triangles below.

Diamonds

Draw a line around each of the four sides to create diamonds below.

Circles

Draw a line around the objects to create circles below.

Ovals

Draw a line around the objects to create ovals below.

Shapes Practice

Using what you have learned, draw along the dotted lines below to create lots of different shapes.

Shapes Practice

Shapes Practice

Here are some more shapes for you to draw.
Remember to try your hardest to follow the lines.

Shapes Practice

Shapes Practice

This bus needs some windows. Can you draw them in?

How many shapes can you find and draw on this boat?

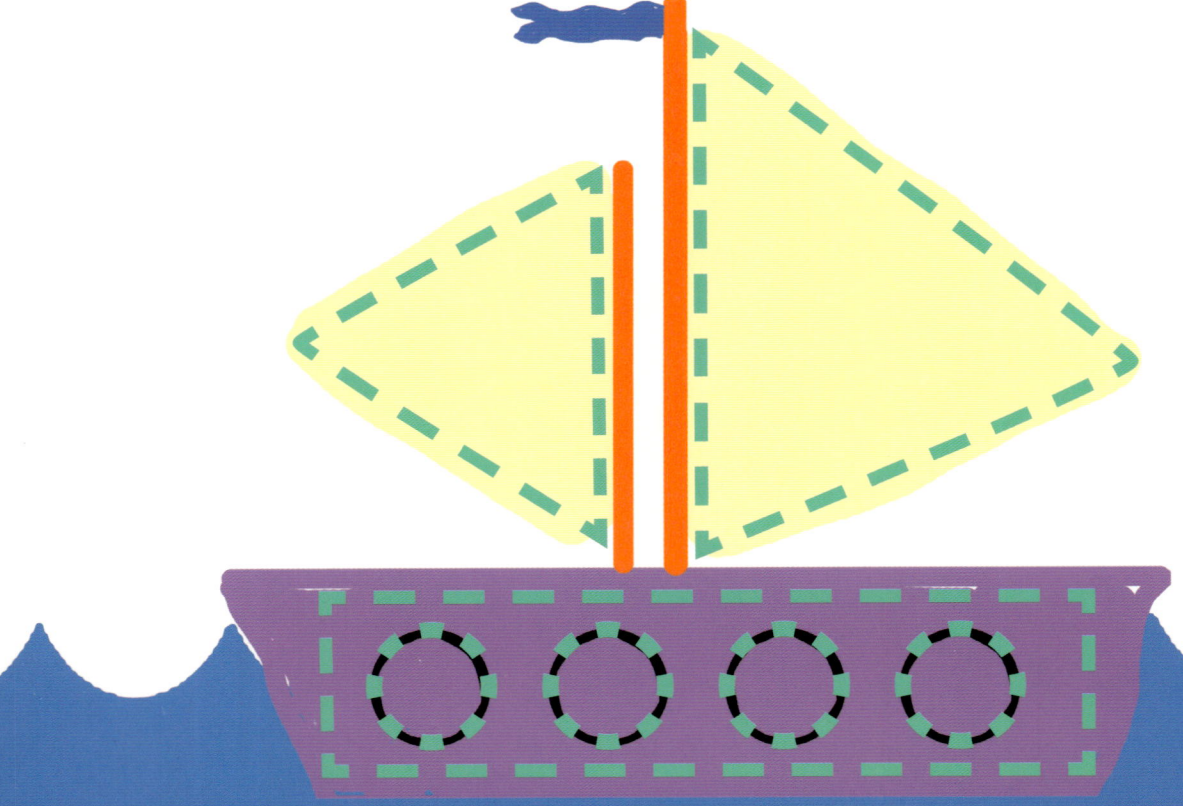

Shapes Practice

Peas are good for you, but you need other food, too.
Draw your favorite foods on this plate. What shapes are they?

Lowercase Letters

We use letters all the time when we write. Use your pen to trace over the dotted lines below to practice writing these letters of the alphabet.

I like my letters in the mail!

Lowercase Letters

Lowercase Letters

Use your pen to trace over the dotted lines
below to practice writing these letters of the alphabet.

Which letter is your favorite?

Lowercase Letters

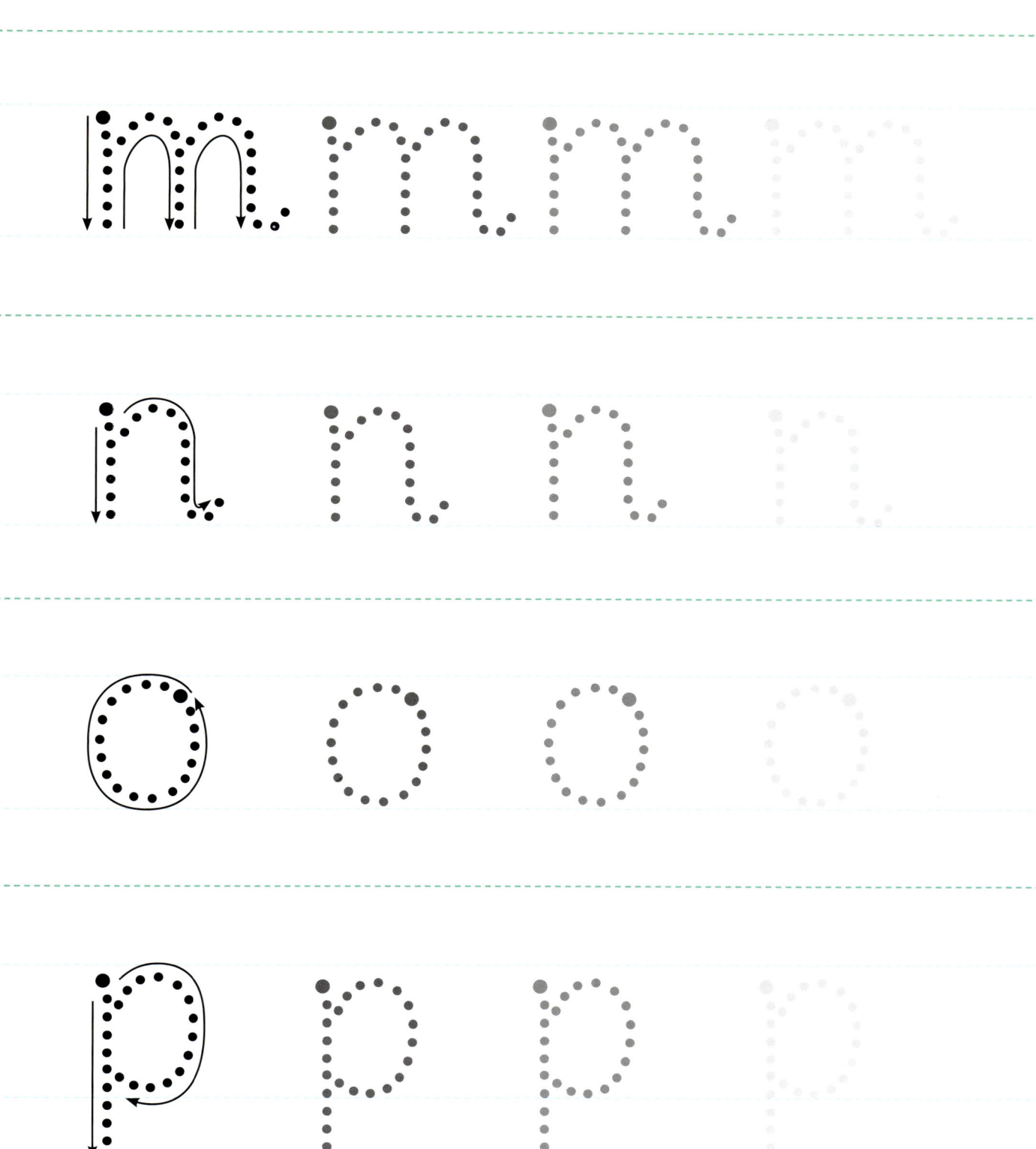

Lowercase Letters

Use your pen to trace over the dotted lines
below to practice writing these letters of the alphabet.

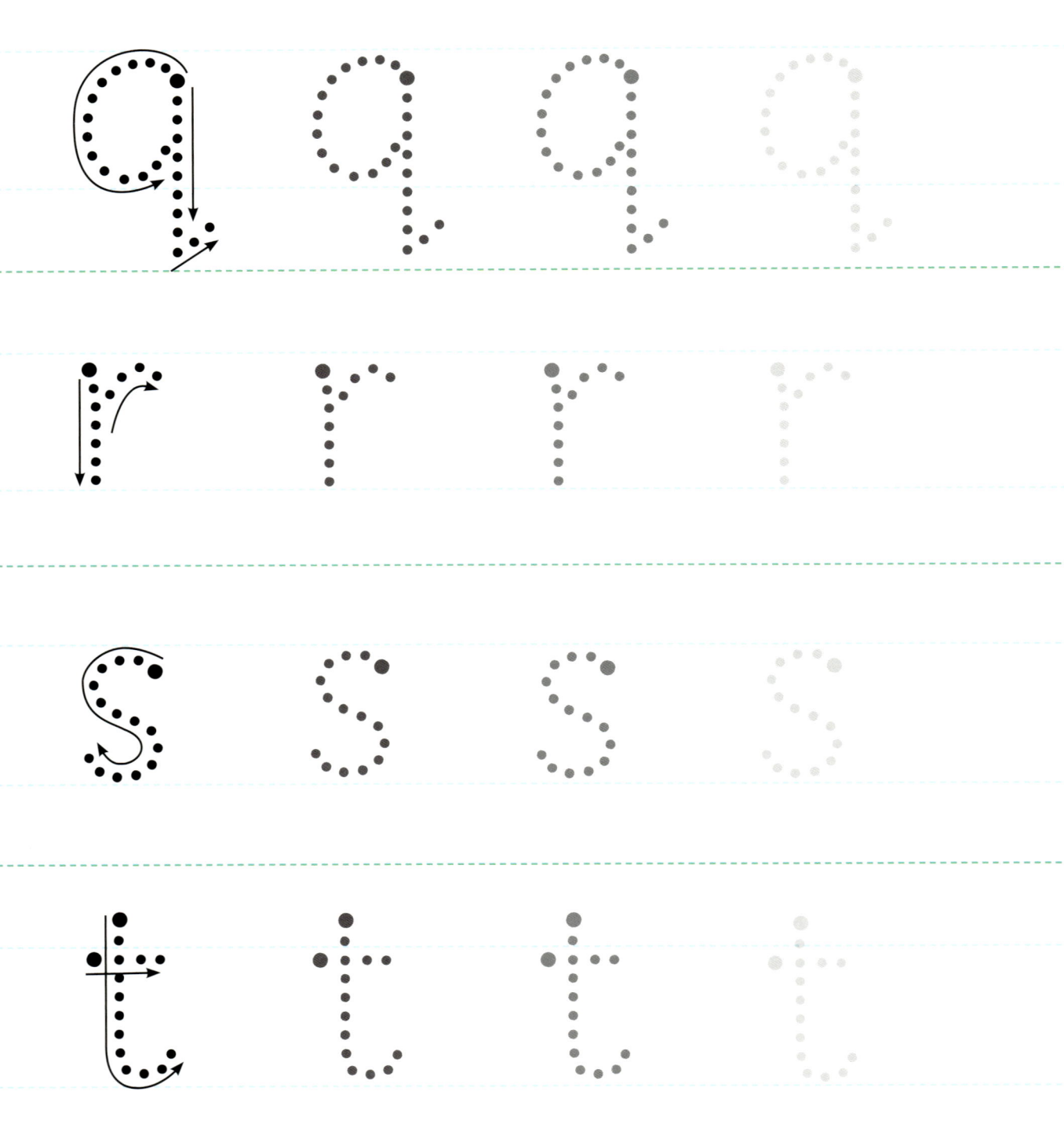

Lowercase Letters

Keep going. You're almost there!

Uppercase Letters

Uppercase letters are used at the start of sentences and when writing names. Use your pen to trace over the dotted lines below to practice writing these letters of the alphabet.

Uppercase Letters

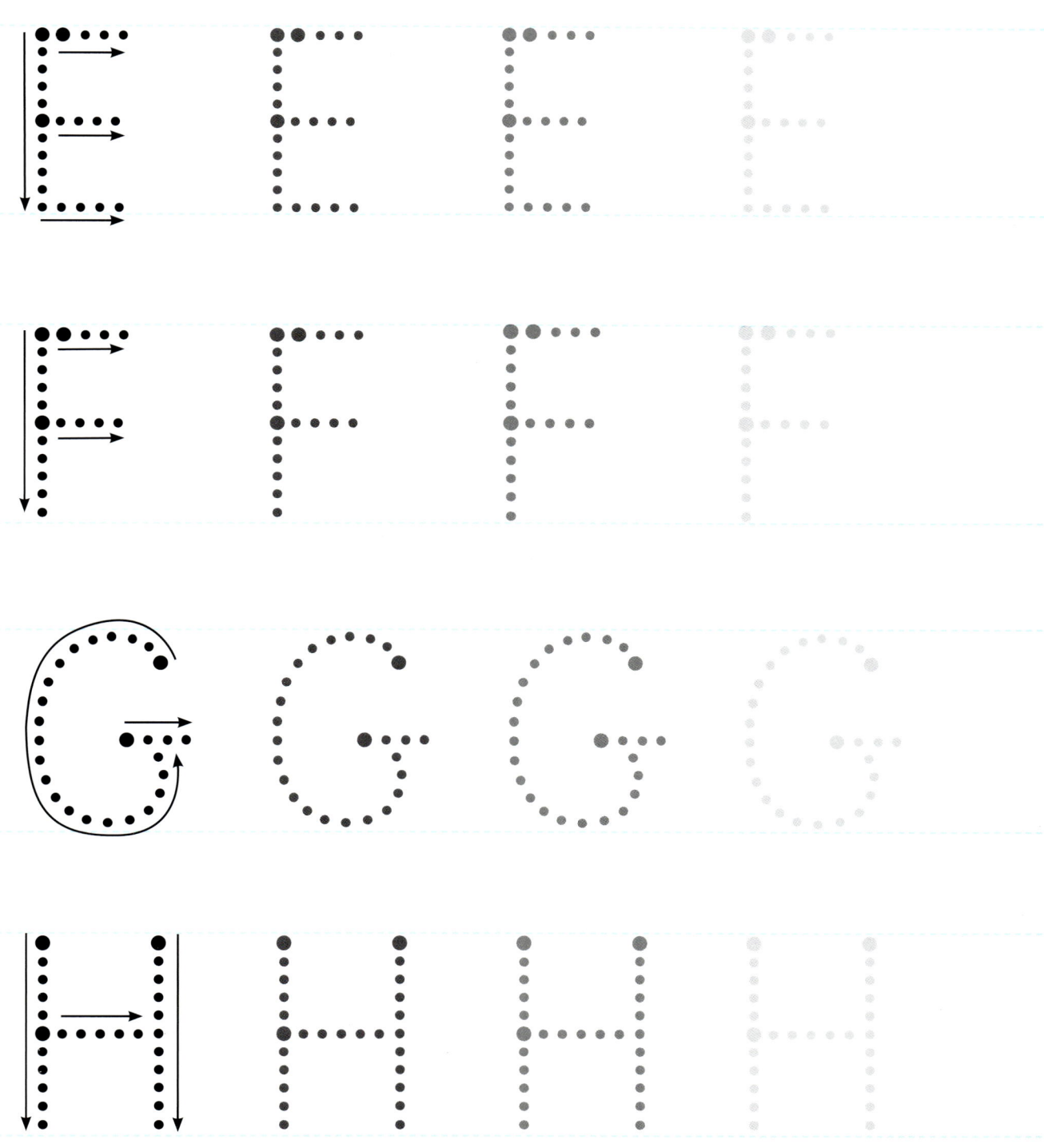

Uppercase Letters

Use your pen to trace over the dotted lines
below to practice writing these letters of the alphabet.

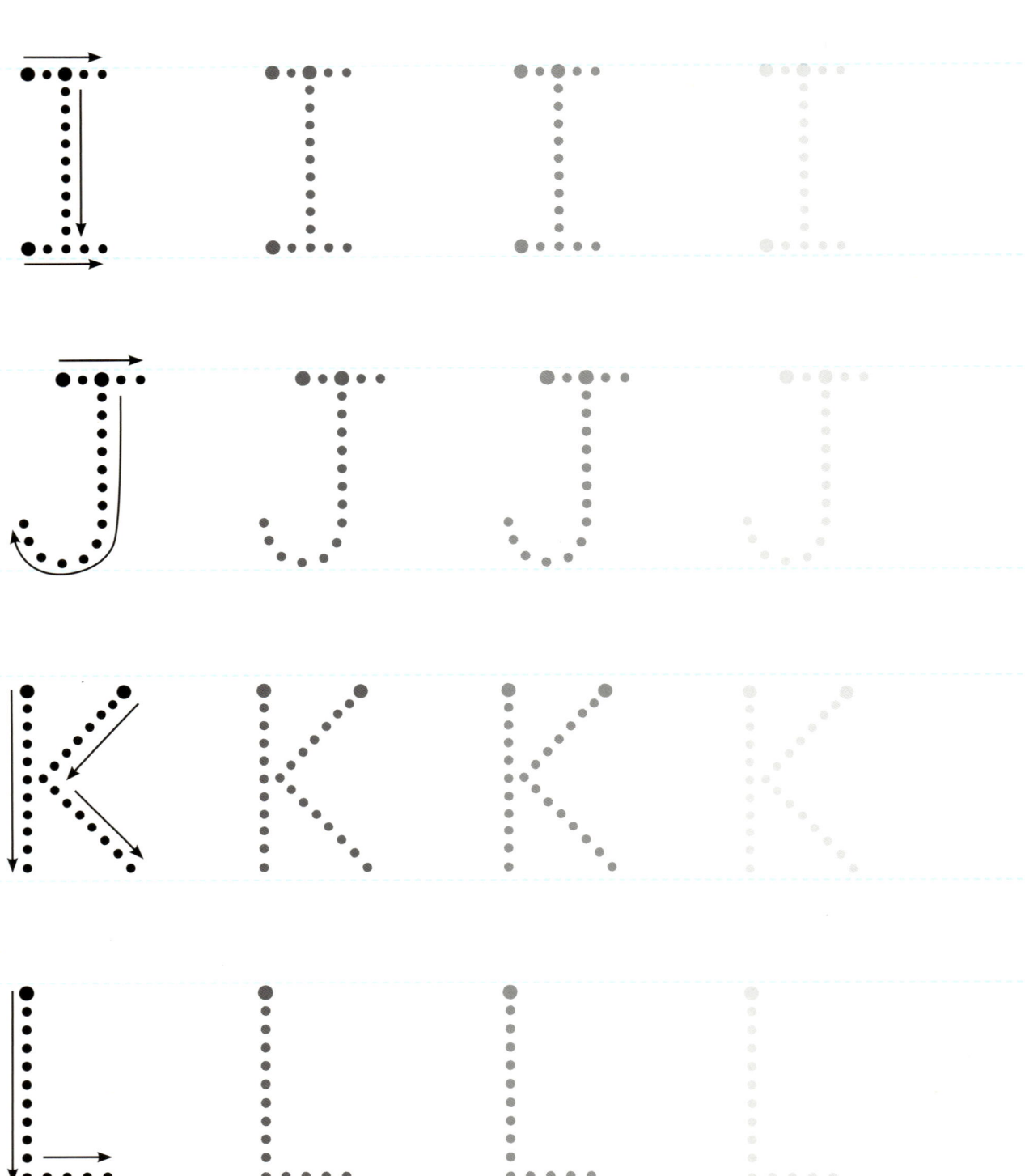

Uppercase Letters

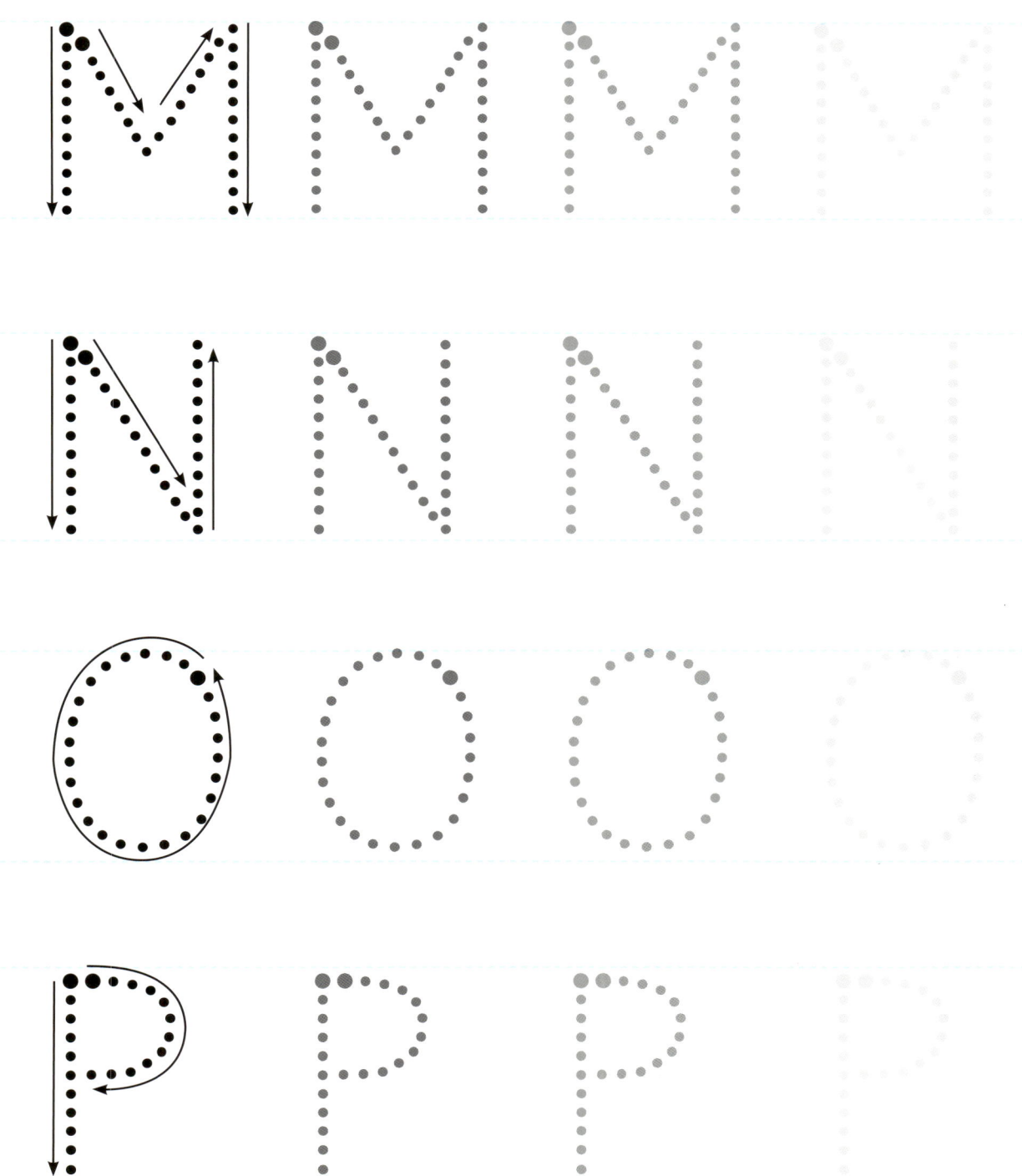

Uppercase Letters

Use your pen to trace over the dotted lines
below to practice writing these letters of the alphabet.

Uppercase Letters

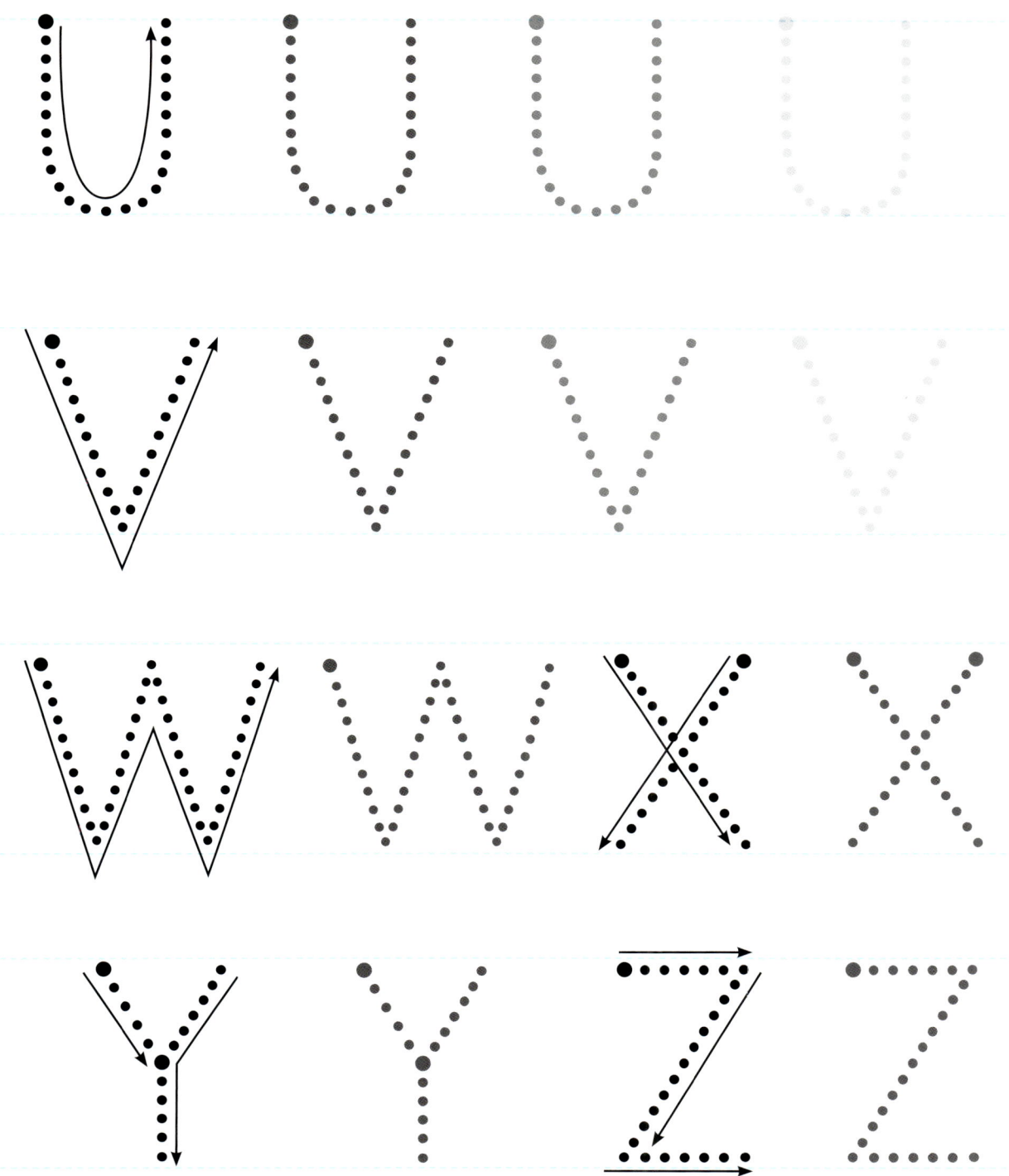

Three-Letter Words

Now you are confident writing the alphabet, use your pen to practice writing these three-letter words.

sun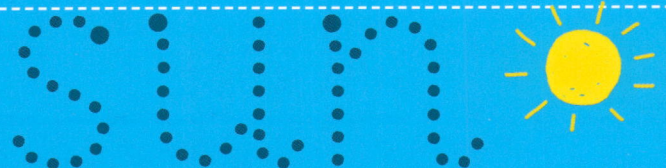

cat

bag

bus

Owl is also a three-letter word.

Three-Letter Words

cup

dog

bee

hat

Four-Letter Words

Use your pen to practice
writing these four-letter words.

moon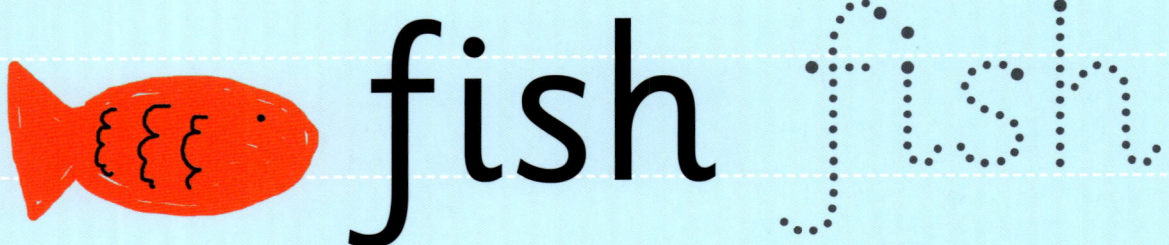

 fish fish

boat boat

 cake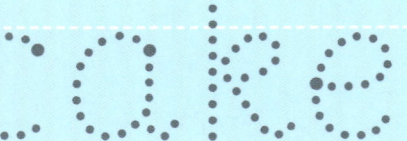

Four-Letter Words

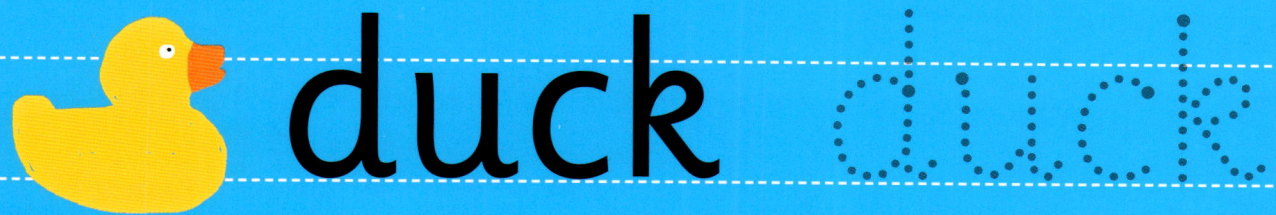

duck duck

sock sock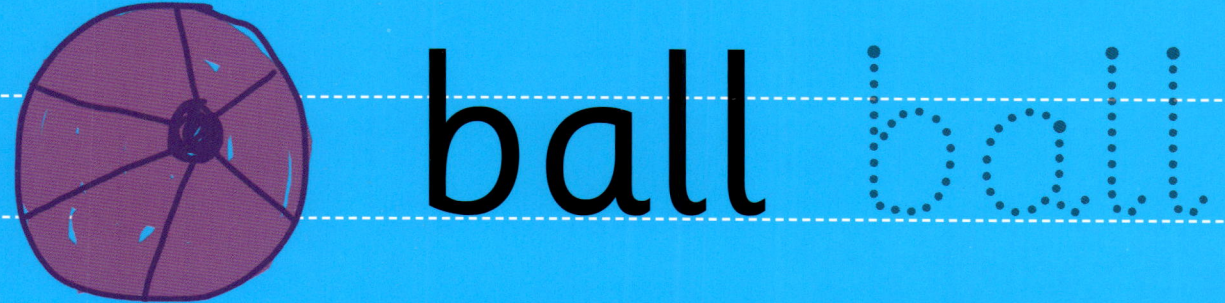

ball ball

star star

Five-Letter Words

Use your pen to practice
writing these five-letter words.

clock

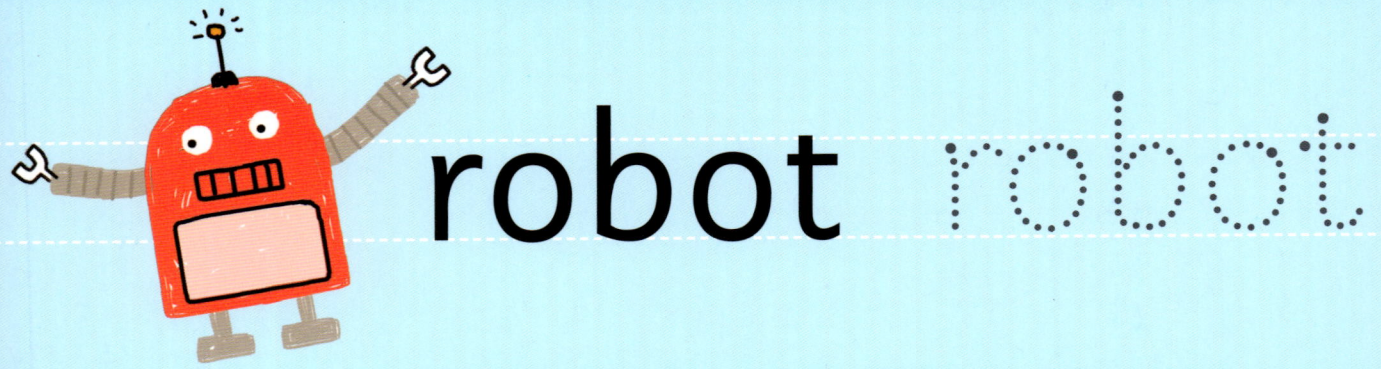

robot robot

chair chair

 house house

Five-Letter Words

mouse mouse

apple apple

plane plane

candy candy

Describing and Naming Words

Practice handwriting by using your pen
to trace over these describing and naming words.

yellow star

purple ball
purple ball

brown chair
brown chair

big house
big house